# A Dictionary of Silly Words About Growing Up

*Written for Parents Who Never Understand Anything Anyway*

By Henry Beard and Roy McKie

*Workman Publishing New York*

# note

I would just like to say that the idea for this book and much encouragement and editorial advice were provided by Christopher B. Cerf, whose support, kind efforts and generous investment of time I am very grateful for. And so, if Chris has been a little late in returning your calls recently, or if he hasn't been prompt to a meeting or if he has been tardy in handing something in, he should be excused, because he was helping Roy and me with this project. Thank you.

Henry Beard

Copyright © 1988 by Henry Beard and Roy McKie

All rights reserved. No portion of this book may be reproduced – mechanically, electronically, or by any other means, including photocopying – without written permission by the publisher.

Library of Congress Cataloging-in-Publication Data

Beard, Henry.
   A dictionary of silly words about growing up
   1. Child development – Humor. 2. Children – Humor.
I. Title.
PN6231.C32B43 1988     818′.5402     87-40643
ISBN 0-89480-584-3
ISBN 0-89480-628-9 (pbk.)

Design: Charles Kreloff

Workman Publishing
708 Broadway
New York, New York 10003

Manufactured in the United States of America
First printing May 1988
10 9 8 7 6 5 4 3 2 1

# accident

Something that happened by mistake and probably would have happened all by itself even if you weren't there and that wasn't your fault because someone would have made you do it if you had done it, which you didn't.

**adult** A very old child with a huge allowance, easy homework and no bedtime.

**adventure**

Something amazing and exciting and fantastic that happened to you or something dull and dopey that happened to somebody else.

**advice** A piece of wisdom from a person who probably first heard and ignored it a long time before you were born.

**afraid** What people sometimes wrongly think other people are just because they suddenly had to look for something under the bed, or made a kind of squeaky burp because of something they ate, or felt like practicing the 100-yard dash right at that moment.

**age** How old you are in years, or your shoe size multiplied by your height in feet, whichever is larger.

# allowance

Money that parents give to children. Depending on the child's age, the amounts most often given are: Too Little (6 to 8 years old); Nowhere Near Enough (8 to 10 years old); and You've Got To Be Kidding (over 10 years old).

# angry

How you feel when someone gives you a present and it's nice and heavy, but it doesn't rattle at all when you shake it, and when you open it up, it isn't a terrific toy like a laser gun or a set of colored pens, it's underwear or socks, or some stupid book like this one.

**animal** One of the four things that everything is one of. The other three are vegetable, mineral and dessert.

**apology** A statement with the words "I'm sorry" in it, made by someone who is too honest to lie, too brave to make excuses and too smart to try to blame it on the dog.

**aunt** Someone who has the same kind of great inside dirt on one of your parents that your sister has on you.

## baby
Cute little thing that smiles a lot of the time because it has never heard of the words "dentist," "vegetable" and "bath."

## baby-sitter
Someone who is paid to make sure that small children get back to sleep after being repeatedly woken up by phone calls from worried parents.

# barbershop

A place where, after you come out and look in the mirror, the only way you can tell that it's your hair is because it's on top of your head.

# bedroom
A place where, if it has only one person in it, the person can't get to sleep because the pile of clothes on the chair looks like a multiple murderer with a chain saw, and if it has two or more people in it, they can't get to sleep because they keep each other awake arguing over whether it looks more like a multiple murderer with a chain saw or an alien lizard-being with a disintegrator pistol.

# bedtime
One-half hour after the absolute latest that homework can be delayed to, and one-half hour before the first good program comes on TV.

# behavior The way you act when people are looking.

**bla-vongo** The way you act when they aren't.

# borrowing A very slow form of theft.

**child** Someone who still remembers what strained peas taste like.

**chore** *1.* A job you have to do around the house. *2.* A daily task. *3.* A kind of work you do to earn your allowance. *4.* A chance to learn discipline. *5.* A way to show that you are responsible. *6.* Phooey.

**clean up** To take everything off the floor and put it away in a place where, in order to find anything, you have to take everything out and put it on the floor.

**closet** A mess with a door on it.

**cousins** Relatives you're supposed to get along with because they're the children of the brothers or sisters your parents never got along with.

**discussion** What adults call a fight. If they scream, shout and slam doors, it's a disagreement. If they throw things, it's a misunderstanding.

# divorce

An event that starts out just like a wedding, since people say silly things, everybody cries, it costs a lot, and it takes for- ever, but afterwards you don't get a toaster oven from your aunt and nobody ever asks to look at the photographs.

# doctor

Someone who gets sick people well enough to sue.

BECAUSE.....

**excuse** *1.* A very good reason why you did something you weren't supposed to do or didn't do something you were. *2.* A not so good reason, shouted from inside a locked bathroom.

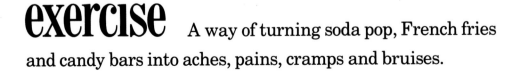

**exercise** A way of turning soda pop, French fries and candy bars into aches, pains, cramps and bruises.

# explanation

A feature-length excuse, with sound effects, a good story, great acting and, if necessary, tears.

## fact

Anything that would have been absolutely true if it hadn't been exaggerated, changed around so it happened to you, or made up entirely.

# fairy tale

A ridiculous story in which no one ever goes to school or has glasses or braces, and everyone wears weird clothes but no one makes fun of them, and at the end the bully is cut up into a million pieces by a guy with a big sword they'd give you the electric chair just for owning and everybody else gets their own bedroom, a huge allowance and a horse.

**falsehood** A big lie, such as "My father is the President of Brazil and a close personal friend of the Pope." *See* FIB.

**family** A group of people who probably would have ended up liking each other if they had gotten together under more favorable circumstances, like at a federal prison or in a train wreck.

# father
The person who, when you do anything really wrong, says your mother has something to speak to you about. *See* MOTHER.

**father's day** Day in June on which dads go outside, and if they see their own shadows, it will be six more weeks before the screens get put up.

**fib** A small lie, such as "My father is the President of Brazil, but he only met the Pope a couple of times."

**fight** An argument over something nobody said or did that takes place between two kids who weren't even there when somebody else started it.

**friend** Anyone who knows your nickname and what your middle initial stands for but never tells either one to anybody else.

**game** An argument with rules.

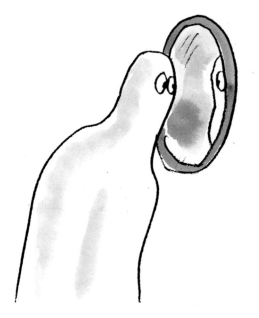

# ghosts

Weird, horrible things that play a big part in the scary stories that adults sometimes tell children about the awful days before cable television and satellite dishes.

# grandparents

The nice old people who helped out with the driving when your parents came from that strange planet they were born on.

# guidance

1. Blah.
2. Blah-blah. 3. Blah-blah-blah.

# health food

The food they serve in hell.

# heart

The part of the body that pumps blood. A long time ago, everyone thought the heart was what made people fall for girlfriends or boyfriends, but modern scientists have found that dumb feelings of love come from the empty space in most people's heads where their brains are supposed to be.

**home** An indoor place containing two or more people who have to go to the bathroom at the same time.

**homework** A nightmare you have before you go to sleep.

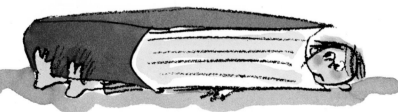

**honest** Being like George Washington, who came right out and told his father he should be punished for cutting down the cherry tree because it was all his idea, even though his brother Samuel sharpened the hatchet and did most of the actual chopping.

**if** A small word that parents add to promises to turn them into excuses.

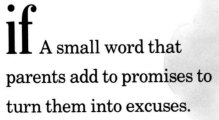

# imagination
Being able to think of things that haven't appeared on TV yet.

# imitate
To copy something you probably thought of first anyway.

# intelligence
Knowing when it's smart to pretend to be stupid.

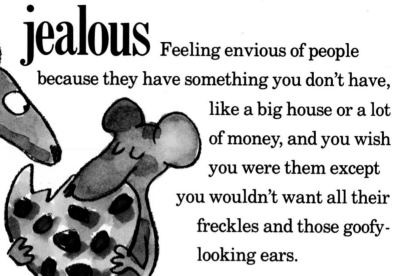

**jealous** Feeling envious of people because they have something you don't have, like a big house or a lot of money, and you wish you were them except you wouldn't want all their freckles and those goofy-looking ears.

**jungle gym** Thing in a playground which you shouldn't feel too bad if you're always falling off of, because if you look around you'll see that there just aren't a whole lot of people getting paid $50,000 a year for hanging upside down from a metal bar.

**kid** *1.* Slang term for child. Its real meaning is "young goat," and so a child's father is an "old goat," which is a name that dads love to be called. *2.* To fool someone.

**leader** The person who, when something goes wrong, has to decide who gets the blame.

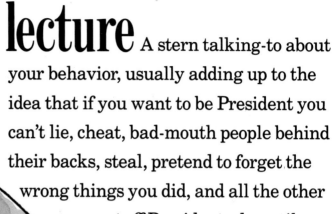

# lecture
A stern talking-to about your behavior, usually adding up to the idea that if you want to be President you can't lie, cheat, bad-mouth people behind their backs, steal, pretend to forget the wrong things you did, and all the other stuff Presidents do until *after* you get into the White House.

**lie** To tell something completely true that accidentally didn't exactly happen.

**lonely** Not having anyone hanging around to complain about being forced to spend time with.

**lose** To put something of yours in a place where you know exactly where it is, except somebody moved it, or borrowed it, or washed it, or took it and then sneaked it back, or put you in a weird trance and made you leave it where it was found by someone who probably stole it in the first place.

**manners**
Knowing which fork to use to jab your little brother or sister with.

**math** What you need to learn so that when you start earning an income, you'll be able to add up the same column of numbers six times in a row and come up with a half-dozen different tax deductions.

**model** Someone who is held up as an example of the right way to be or to do something; a creep; a jerk; a fink; a rat; a louse; a turkey.

**money** Something adults always say can't buy happiness, which is probably true since the amounts they hand it out in wouldn't even add up to a down payment on a giggle.

**mother** The person who, when you do anything really wrong, says your father wants to talk to you about something. *See* FATHER.

# moving
Going to live in a place where there are new kids who haven't heard your best jokes, new neighbors who haven't seen through your most amazing excuses, and new reasons why you should get a bigger allowance.

## neighbor's kid
Strange form of life that combines the manners of a garbage disposal with the brains of a medium-size houseplant.

## neighbor's other kid
What the stuff in the bottom of the aquarium wants to be when it grows up.

**nightmare** The only really scary stuff you can watch without being accompanied by an adult.

**no** *1.* Maybe. *2.* Perhaps. *3.* We'll see. *4.* Ask your mother. *5.* Yes.

# older brother

Someone who can't help you with your homework because he's already forgotten everything you're trying to learn.

# older sister

Someone who can't help you with your homework because she's helping her boyfriend with his.

**parents** A man and a woman who had the brains and good taste to have someone like you instead of one of those jerky kids who are in all the commercials on TV.

**politeness** Not saying to adults the kinds of things they say to you.

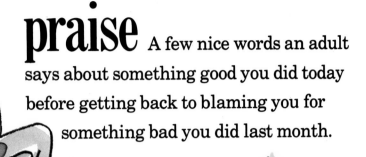

**praise** A few nice words an adult says about something good you did today before getting back to blaming you for something bad you did last month.

**prize** A compliment you have to find a place in the closet for.

**promptness** Getting to places on time so you'll have a couple of hours to make a rocketship out of paper clips or train a bug to jump rope before whoever you're going to meet shows up or whatever was supposed to happen starts.

# punishment Something bad that's done to you so you'll learn the important lesson that if you're going to break the rules, you should work very hard and earn a lot of money so you can afford a really smart lawyer.

# quarter A coin that adults think is enough for you to be able to get ten pounds of candy and a couple of dozen comic books and still have some left over to buy a pair of ice skates, a bicycle and a savings bond.

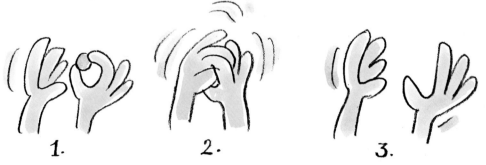

1.       2.       3.

**relatives** Any people you hate before you meet them.

# remarriage
A situation in which a family that could really use a backup TV, a second car in case the first one breaks, or an extra stereo for upstairs, gets a spare mother or father instead.

# report card
Piece of paper on which grades are written. Even big-shot scientists can't explain why, but when a report card is carried home from school, it attracts bolts of lightning, sudden gusts of wind and small meteors, and is the favorite food of wild dogs, even more than steak.

# reward
Praise you can spend.

**rule** The only thing that doesn't make a noise or a mess when you break it, but you still get punished.

**school** A place where you go to learn the math and writing skills you'll need as an adult to complain about the education budget and send angry letters to the teachers' association.

**secret** Something that only one person knows, and he or she forgot it.

**sibling** An old-fashioned word for a brother or sister. No one knows for sure what ancient language it came from, but it might be Latin (*sibla* = a loud noise, a big crash); Babylonian (*ziblik* = to pelt, to sock, to slug, to pummel); Greek  (*syblos* = awful, terrible, horrible, hopeless); Old English (*sibbel* = broken, lost, missing, wet); German (*zieblung* = a pest, a brother, a nuisance); or Celtic (*soeblig* = I didn't, you did, I won't, you will).

**sick** Not feeling well, or holding the medical thermometer under hot water when no one is looking.

**sit** What will be painful to do if you're caught pulling that thermometer trick.

**steal** To take things from other people without their permission when you're not working for the government.

# stepparent

A brand-new mother or father brought to your home by a confused or crazy stork.

# tantrum

*1.* A slight display of anger. *2.* All right, a sort of blow-up or a kind of ranting rage. *3.* Okay, okay, a screaming, shouting, jumping-up-and-down fit.

*4.* Well, if you don't like it, come up with your own crummy definition, smarty pants! And I hope you get a paper cut from this page and the book falls on your head and knocks you out cold!

**threat** The only promise made by adults that they always keep.

**time** How long something takes or the exact moment when it happens. Time is measured in seconds, minutes, hours, days, weeks, months and years, and some common time periods are: the one-minute TV commercial (190 seconds); the hour in math class (115 minutes); the hour at a friend's house (11 minutes); Monday (44 hours); Saturday (9 hours); January (32 weeks); July (4 days); and the first year of school (740 months).

**truth** What really happened, more or less, with the part about the Martians knocking over the fishbowl with blasto rays left out.

**uncle** A man who proves that you don't have to be just like your parents, since after all, one of them had someone as weird as him for a brother.

**vacation** A trip to some place where no one can remember when it rained so much.

**vet** A doctor whose patients can't sue, unless the parrot talks.

**want** *1.* Need. *2.* Must get right away. *3.* Absolutely have to have. *4.* Cannot possibly live without. *5.* Probably will actually die or something right this minute if I do not receive.

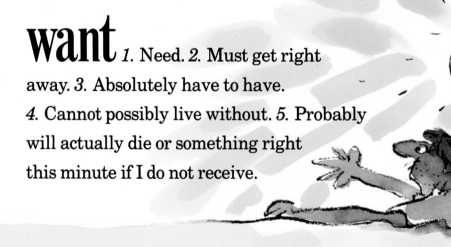

**wish** Something you want to happen or be different; for example, a birthday wish, like "I wish I didn't have to put out a major fire before I get to eat this cake."

**x-ray** The only really ugly picture of you that doesn't get framed and put in the living room.

**younger brother**
Someone who can't help you with your homework because his computer is broken.

## younger sister

One of only two people in the world who think you know everything.

## yourself

The other one.

**zebra** A horse whose clothes were picked out by its mother.